michelle m

Author of **SASS**

THE

Sassy

Girl's

Checklist
for Living,
Loving, &
Overcoming

HARVEST HOUSE PUBLISHERS

EUGENE, OREGON

Published in association with the literary agency of Alive Communications, Inc., 7680 Goddard Street, Ste #200, Colorado Springs, CO 80920. www.alivecommunications.com.

Cover by Koechel Peterson & Associates, Inc., Minneapolis, Minnesota

Cover photo © Tom Henry / Koechel Peterson & Associates, Minneapolis, Minnesota

THE SASSY GIRL'S CHECKLIST FOR LIVING, LOVING, AND OVERCOMING
Copyright © 2007 by Michelle McKinney Hammond
Published by Harvest House Publishers
Eugene, Oregon 97402
www.harvesthousepublishers.com

Library of Congress Cataloging-in-Publication Data
McKinney Hammond, Michelle, 1957-
The sassy girl's checklist for living, loving, and overcoming / Michelle McKinney Hammond.
    p. cm.
ISBN-13: 978-0-7369-1827-5 (pbk.)
ISBN-10: 0-7369-1827-2
    1. Bible. O.T. Proverbs XXXI—Devotional use. 2. Christian women—Conduct of life.
3. Conduct of life—Biblical teaching. I. Title.
BS1465.54.M35 2007
248.8'43—dc22

                                                                    2006022936

Printed in the United States of America

        07 08 09 10 11 12 13 14 15 / VP-SK / 10 9 8 7 6 5 4 3 2 1

To every sassy woman in search of
a higher level of living.
Here's to owning our stuff and doing
what's necessary to reach our goal.

Acknowledgments

To my Harvest House family—Simply, I love you and appreciate all that you do.

Beth Justino—Thanks for not only working so hard on my behalf but being a great sounding board and a treasure chest of wisdom.

To all the sassy women in my life (you know who you are)—Without you I wouldn't be as sassy! Love to all and unending thanks.

Contents

Building Up Others
153

Inner Strength
163

Generosity
173

Master Checklist
181

You Are Priceless

We see them everywhere—the MasterCard ads and billboards telling us the value of specific items and then concluding with the idea that truly it is the intangible things in life that are priceless. The same can be said of women. The price tag attached to the things that make us beautiful and desirable on the outside can range from the inexpensive to the outrageous, but it is the nature and character of a woman, the indefinable essence of who she is, that makes her priceless. I imagine that if MasterCard were to devote one of its advertisements to women it would go something like this:

Fabulous tresses	$ 150
Amazing black dress	$ 300
Designer shoes	$ 350
A really great watch	$ 500
Diva bling	$ 2500
The essence of a divine woman	Priceless

It's true that though there are certain diva staples every woman in the know has in her closet, it is the very thing that cannot be purchased that makes her priceless to her loved ones, her community, and to the world at large. Like the world's costliest fragrance made from countless flowers crushed to extract the rare oils, so it is that every sassy diva becomes the sum of the priceless fruit that has been deposited in her from her vast array of experiences that have taught her lessons and seasoned her character with grace. When squeezed by the situations and circumstances of life, her essence grows sweeter and blesses everyone around her with its fragrance.

For the most part no one will ever be bold enough to tell you what is missing from your internal toilette. You must claim the responsibility of "checking yourself," so to speak, and cultivating your mind, your heart, and your spirit to line up with the divine attributes and fruits that will make you so rarely you—you, the life-giver, the nurturer, the sister, the friend, the wife, the mother, the quiet influencer who causes invisible revolutions with a mere touch, look, inflection, or suggestion.

Woman, do you know how powerful you really are? How valuable you are? Only a true sassy girl knows for sure. She never settles for one level of living. She always aspires to know, be, and do better. A sassy girl continually takes her own temperature and heart rate and challenges herself to grow beyond where she presently stands. She is constantly up for promotion and expansion beyond her personal borders. Removing the limits, finding and tapping new inner strength and a greater understanding of who God created her to be provokes her to bear and share richer fare with those who surround her. We find the perfect example of this divine principle being lived out when we examine the life and attributes of the ultimate sassy girl, the woman found in Proverbs 31. Her life gives us a clear-cut road map we can follow to reach our destination: of rejoicing in being all that God created us to be, a loving testament of His excellence, glory, and power.

On that note I have to ask: Are you up to the challenge, girl?

Are you ready, willing, and able to do the work it takes to go to the next level of partaking of the divine nature of God and manifesting that as only a true diva can? Are you willing to check yourself and make the changes necessary to perfect the art of being a woman according to God's design? Of being sassy, saved, and oh so successful in every area of your life? Then get ready, roll up your pretty sleeves, and let's begin.

1 *Embrace Your Season*

Who can find a virtuous woman?
for her price is far above rubies.

PROVERBS 31:10 KJV

*O*ften quoted but not commonly seen, the search is on for the virtuous woman. *Chokmah* is the Hebrew word used to describe a woman of excellence, one who has mastered the art of skillful living. Skillful living hints at perfecting the delicate balance of the components of life so that each is performed well. No "jack of all trades and master of none" stuff going on here. Each area of life has been approached from a place of discipline and thoughtful consideration to the timing, logistics, and even the consequences of each choice. Faith has been supplemented with virtue because of the knowledge acquired to impart self-control, which ultimately leads to godliness with great gain, which in turn releases you to walk in unconditional love toward all you encounter.

But more than that, the art of skillful living has to do with having an understanding of the seasons of your life and the purpose for each season. This was the essential key to the excellence spoken of by Bathsheba, the wife of King David of Israel, to encourage her son Solomon in what to look for when seeking a wife. Whether you are married or single, you must be cognizant of the fact that timing is everything, although it's aligned equally with attitude. Our attitudes shape our words, which shape our actions. Those actions become habits that form our character. Our character determines our destiny—a destiny that can be filled with blessings or curses based on our choices.

At the end of the day our Proverbs 31 lady was blessed by her husband and her children, and probably by her co-laborers and her community. She created a legacy that was far-reaching by aligning herself according to God's design and allowing His plan to unfold beautifully in the fabric of her life. The end result was an amazing tapestry that must have made God smile, which released favor and blessing into her life emotionally, materially, and spiritually.

Getting our priorities in order and choosing to focus on what is relevant for the hour and season we are in is crucial to having a systematic plan that works for our lives. God is a God of order. It is in that order that excellence is found. He created the seasons to reflect the cycle of our own lives. Truly there is a time for planting, a time of harvest, a time for eating the fruits of our labor, and a time for dying to give way to new and sweeter fruit. This cycle is present in every area of our lives—emotionally, relationally, financially, professionally, even spiritually. As we embrace our seasons, understanding their purpose and looking forward to the blessings on the other side of them, we are able to weather the transitions gracefully and reap a bountiful harvest from each one.

So what does that mean for you right where you are today? Well, if you are single, rejoice and take full advantage of all that is solely yours. Take advantage of the time, space, and resources you have to explore and enjoy every aspect of life. Be aware that seasons do pass, so plant well while you have everything at your disposal to do so.

Are you a newlywed? Rejoice in the honeymoon period of your life. This is a critical time for you to put certain things in place to secure your marriage. You help set the course of your future by what you pour into the heart of your husband in these early stages of becoming one. Build honor, trust, unity, and security. Make yourself a haven for him, one whom he looks forward to running home to. Create habits now that will help lay the solid foundation your marriage will stand on. This is the beginning of the rest of your life. Build your house well.

Are you a new mother? Rejoice in this time that goes by so quickly. Take all the time you need to nurture that new, beautiful life and find your identity in the power of motherhood. After all, that precious little boy or girl might become a world leader based on your input and preparation. It is an awesome task and privilege to be responsible for the gift God puts in your care. Make mothering one of your primary priorities. Look forward to seeing your handiwork flourish into full bloom.

Are you a wife beyond your honeymoon years? Yours is the privilege of experiencing many incredible seasons—some warm, some hot, some cold—all of them occasions for greater growth and greater rewards if you weather each season well. Purpose to always be fruitful no matter what. Continue planting, watering, fertilizing, and harvesting. But also know when to rest and embrace the transitions, keeping in mind that the end goal is to bear fruit that remains, that leaves an indelible print of love and godliness on the lives you touch.

Are you a businesswoman? An entrepreneur? Plant carefully and prepare to reap what you have sown. Be a wise steward of your increase. Like the ant, be aware of the season for harvesting and storing and trust God to fill your storehouse to overflowing for the purpose of being able to pour out to others in need.

Are you an empty nester? In retirement? A widow? Look beyond yourself to see a field ripe for harvesting. There comes a time when the experiences we've gained, along with rewards both spiritual and financial, bring us to the place of benevolence. Where we use what God has given us to bless others. This is truly the greatest season—the full fruition of our labor manifesting one of the greatest blessings of all, the privilege of giving wholeheartedly.

To everything there is a season and a purpose. As we accept this truth and learn to embrace where we are, we grow in grace and in the sufficiency of all that we need in that season to walk in excellence. Two impulses we must resist are to lag behind and to grow impatient with where we are. Only you know which season you are in and what your attitude is toward that season. Begin now to take stock of where you are and how you view yourself in light of that knowledge. Then step up to the diva-licious challenge of being all that you were created to be—a woman of excellence, thriving in her purpose according to God's divine timing.

> A good name is more desirable
> than great riches; to be esteemed is
> better than silver or gold.
> PROVERBS 22:1

Check Yourself

- Do you walk in excellence? What do you do?

- How would you score yourself on a scale from one to ten, with one being in great shape, in the following areas?
    - spiritually   ____
    - emotionally   ____
    - physically   ____
    - financially   ____
    - relationally   ____
- Which area could use improvement?

- What are your strengths in this area? Weaknesses?

- What three steps can you take toward improving in this area?

   1.

   2.

   3.

Personal Thoughts & Meditations

---

*W*hat do people say about you? If you overheard them talking about you, would you want to know and befriend that person? You can't please all of the people all of the time, so how do you find the balance for living a life that curries favor with those you encounter versus sacrificing who you really are in order to be a people pleaser? The secret is in first living to please God. The fruit of this selective living will be favor with those around you. Pursuing peace and walking in love are huge. And there's no room for pride or being defensive. The catch-22 about pride is it eventually always makes you look like a fool. While you are busy posturing and promoting a specific image of yourself, people are seeing through the facade and forming negative conclusions about your character.

Replace defensive living with offensive and positive positioning. Seek to give what you want to receive no matter what. Don't take things personally. Most of the time whatever is going on around you and the reactions you encounter have very little to do with you. The response has to do with the accumulation of many experiences that particular person had before he or she even got to you. With this in mind, seek to bless that person instead of struggling to regain your own footing. Mastering this one thing will give you tremendous victory in the area of relationships. As you make pleasing God your goal, which includes His command to love your neighbor as you love yourself, the fruit of this decision becomes obvious: a legacy of good will. But most of all you will garner the pleasure of your heavenly Father, who just happens to be a King. And when the King smiles, there is favor.

Check Yourself

- What do people say about your character?

- What would you like them to say about you?

- What habits or attitudes do you need to change to get a more desirable review from others?

- If you met yourself at a function, would you want to be your friend? Why or why not?

Personal Thoughts & Meditations

---

*T*he goal we've all been wired in our spirits to achieve is to live a value-added life. We were created to be priceless, to grow and make lasting contributions to the world and to the people around us. We should be a valuable commodity to those who experience life within our personal, social, and professional circles. The things we say and do add or subtract from our lives as well as the lives of others on a daily basis. I believe this is why the Bible tells us to begin with our thought life—to purpose to think on things that are true, honorable, right, pure, lovely, admirable, excellent, and praiseworthy (see Philippians 4:8). If this is what we are predisposed to mentally, our thoughts will manifest for all to see. What proceeds from our mouths as well as our deeds will line up with God's design for us.

How the world longs to see individuals overflowing with integrity! This is what gives people hope. They long to believe that if they live a righteous life the results will be victorious. With so much bad news abounding, many wonder if there is anyone left who will not compromise his or her standards to get ahead in life. People want to see the unlikely suspect, the good guy who stands for what is right, overcome the obstacles of life with grace, humility, and aplomb. Why do we value this so much? Perhaps because this is a confirmation of the greatness of an awesome God and the virtues He extols. When we walk in excellence and integrity, others view a reflection of God. We are an extension of His power and virtue in the earthly realm. We all long to see God, and in a physical sense the way we see Him is in the eyes of people around us. This is valuable to the human spirit because goodness gives us more hope and more faith that God exists and He is truly good.

Check Yourself

- What do you think of yourself?

- Write a description of how you think others describe you.

- How can you reconcile your description of yourself with how others describe you?

- Why are you valuable in the life of your family? To your friends? In your place of employment? At your church?

- Would you like to increase your value to others? What will you do to accomplish this?

Personal Thoughts & Meditations

2 *Loving*

Her husband has full
confidence in her
and lacks nothing of value.
She brings him good,
not harm, all the days of her life

PROVERBS 31:11-12

Sassy

A woman can make or break a man, a child, a nation—anything she touches. This is why a woman needs wisdom. Whether you are married or not, you have a profound effect on the men in your personal universe and beyond. How many men do you know who don't trust women? Who taught them that? Sad to say, another woman did. They were profoundly affected by something they saw or witnessed that cemented this negative conclusion in their minds. Most men walk in fear of women because men sometimes know better than we just how powerful we really are.

Obviously Satan knew the magnitude of our power. It was through the woman that he got the man to sin in the garden. Ever wonder why he didn't go directly to Adam with the fruit? Though both man and woman are equally vulnerable to sin, Satan knew that next to himself, woman was the most persuasive instrument of temptation he would ever be able to utilize. This is why we are constantly encouraged to yield our members to God as instruments of righteousness. The enemy of our souls is always trying to influence us to do evil. The fight is on for our bodies. We cannot serve two masters; therefore, we will love one and hate the other. It behooves us to be cognizant of whom we are surrendering ourselves to.

The spirit of a man is a sensitive thing. Men live for the approval of the women they love. They need to feel honored and respected.

A disrespectful or disdainful attitude can damage them more deeply than we realize. The worse thing a man can feel is failure in the eyes of his woman. He will direct his attention to whomever (or wherever) will affirm him as a success. His heart will trust in the one who gives him nonjudgmental suggestions and speaks the truth in love to him. If he has to guess your motives, he will be uncomfortable with you. The worst disease one can have in a marriage is that of dis-ease…(see how revealing that word can be?). Dis-ease can poison a relationship in record time if not dealt with.

The best prescription for this disease is love, understanding, patience, and assurance. This is the heart of God toward us. He forgives our failings. He looks beyond our faults and sees our need. He stands in the gap when we are weak and becomes our strength without criticizing. He lovingly partners with us in our struggles because He knows we are but dust. So is your man. Keep it in perspective. A man who truly loves you will not try to hurt you or fail you on purpose. The reality is that you and your mate will both fail one another, so purpose to give grace for grace so that both of your hearts can rest in the confidence that in spite of your failings you are loved.

Check Yourself

- How do you nurture trust in the heart of your man? In the hearts of those around you?

- How do you handle sensitive situations or intimate issues with your loved ones?

- Have you proven yourself to be trustworthy and reliable to your loved ones?

- What do you do to make those you love feel safe with you?

- How do you cover the failings of those who disappoint you without enabling them to continue unvictorious habits?

Personal Thoughts & Meditations

―――――――――

*I*t is important to know what men value before you can fill the bill. First, they place value on if they are of value to you. Second, men place tremendous value on the trustworthiness of the woman in their lives. They want to know their hearts and their secrets are safe in your care, that you are a partner, a team player, and a co-conspirator who has his back. This enables him to focus on being the man he should be for you as he operates in integrity and walks uprightly. With your support he can plot his course and know he has value in your life because you validate him on a daily basis.

You validate him not just vocally but by adding empowerment to his life through love, encouragement, a listening ear, and helpful advice. You add to his life by never tearing him down; instead, you always build him up. You assist him by living wisely—and this encompasses all areas: spiritually, physically, financially. Are you getting the picture? You're not creating bills that make him worry how he is going to provide for you. You take care of your body so you are desirable. You cover him with prayer and inspire him to deeper depths in his relationship with God. At the end of the day you add more to his world than he ever thought possible!

Third, men value their manhood being affirmed by their ability to please you materially *and* intimately. Fourth, a secure home environment ranks right up there with the first three.

The emphasis on these four items can change depending on his most immediate need. So the easy list to keep in mind is a man wants to be well respected, well pleased, and well satisfied. (Credit for this wisdom goes to my mentor, P.B. Wilson.)

Perhaps you are not married. This doesn't stop you from operating in the same grace toward the men in your life that look to you as a friend or sister. How about your employer? Your co-workers? This way of living should encompass everyone you meet. Your presence, your friendship, your love should be priceless to those around you because of what you deposit into their lives. Everyone values feeling honored. They should feel richer and fuller for the experience of knowing you. And you should feel more prosperous for having the privilege of being a blessing to others. This is the ultimate in gracious living.

Check Yourself

- How do you add value to the life of your loved ones? Your employers? Your friends?

- What can you do to make others in your life realize their value to you?

- In what ways do you prove yourself to be trustworthy to those in your world?

- How do you exhibit the spirit of being a team player with your friends? Family members? Significant relationships? Co-workers?

- In what ways can you be instrumental in building confidence in the hearts of your loved ones?

Personal Thoughts & Meditations

*A*s you think back on your life, I'm sure you can say with certainty that some relationships were good for you and some were bad for you. While contemplating our own relationships, we must search our hearts and reflect on our own contributions to the lives of others. One Bible translation says that the extraordinary woman spoken of in Proverbs 31 helped her husband and did not hinder him all the days of her life, while another version says she brought him good and not harm.

If it is true that we were created to be helpmeets for our husbands, it stands to reason that we should help them and not be deterrents in their lives. This can manifest in many ways, but I think the first one we must look at is mentally. You, woman of God, need to know that your tone of voice, your attitude, your respect (or lack of it) toward your man helps determine how he views himself. In light of this, what he thinks of himself will dictate how he responds to you as well as to the rest of the world. A woman has the power to revolutionize her man and help him be a positive force in his home, workplace, and community by what she feeds him physically, emotionally, mentally, and spiritually.

It is important to be guided by the Spirit of God and not just your emotions when walking with others in your life, whether they be husband or friend. Choosing to be a force of good in the lives of those who play significant roles in your life will not only empower them but bless you. You will reap the fruit of what you pour into them. If you pour in confidence, their increased productivity will be a blessing to you. If you pour in love, you will glean appreciation and honor from them.

Remember we do reap what we sow, even if it's no more than words or things telegraphed in silence. Take thought to the garden you plant and prepare for the harvest.

Check Yourself

- Do you add to or subtract from the life of your loved ones? In what ways?

- Make a list of the good you contribute to your loved ones and other significant relationships.

- In what ways did you subtract from them in the past? How has this changed?

- In what ways can you be more sensitive to the needs of your husband? Friends? Children? Co-workers? Significant relationships?

- What is the fruit of your relationship with others?

Personal Thoughts & Meditations

3 *Resourcefulness*

She selects wool and flax
and works with eager hands.

PROVERBS 31:13

Resourcefulness is the ability to find what you need to do the task at hand. Whether it is researching a subject to create a better way of doing something, getting others involved in your vision to help you move forward, or simply creatively finding the resources you need to get the job done, resourceful people are never hindered by lack and dead ends. These are foreign concepts to them. They will find the bargain. The substitute. The thing better than what you were expecting. They will find a way to make it happen and ultimately garner success.

Resourcefulness took the clay of the earth and fashioned a man. Then He took the rib from the man and fashioned a woman. Using what was at hand and taking it to another level is what resourcefulness is all about. Every sassy girl masters the intangible by seeing the little things that make up the big picture. One by one she gathers them and fashions them into something beautiful, something lasting, something of value.

Check Yourself

- In what ways are you resourceful?

37

- What are the fruits of resourcefulness?

- In what areas could you be more resourceful?

- In what ways is your resourcefulness a tribute to the creativity of God?

- How can your resourcefulness be a blessing to others?

Personal Thoughts & Meditations

They say that necessity is the mother of invention and a little bit of creativity goes a long way. Creativity and innovation are special gifts that most women seem to possess naturally. Whether it's finding a piece of fabric and fashioning it into something truly beautiful that she can wear, taking broken pieces of glass and turning them into a mosaic, taking the death of a son killed by a drunk driver and creating a movement that inspires national awareness to the dangers of drinking and driving, or working magic over some leftovers and turning it into a stew, women have been making something out of seemingly nothing and transforming tragedies into triumphs since the world began.

The virtue of being able to work with your hands, to touch things with your own special brand of creativity and watch them turn into something that blesses others, is an awesome experience that we all get to have on one level or another. The amazing thing about reveling in the exercise of resourcefulness is this is one of the greatest ways you can reflect the power of God at work in your life. Our God is a creative God. As His children we inherit His nature. One of the greatest gifts we can give Him is that of imitating His nature in order to glorify Him.

Check Yourself

- How creative are you in the way you go about your work?

- What stops you from taking more initiative? How could this hinder you from progressing in life?

- What common characteristics do you see in people who get promoted or elevated?

- In what ways are you able to transform hindrances into opportunities?

• How does your creativity bless others?

Personal Thoughts & Meditations

---

*O*ne can look at a glass and see it as either half full or half empty. Attitude is truly everything. If we are truly working as unto the Lord, we must have a joyous approach to the privilege we have been given to serve in whatever capacity we are able. Remember, someone would probably give a lot to have your job. Because familiarity sometimes breeds contempt, we may lose sight of how blessed we are to have that job, that husband, that child. Someone somewhere is praying for what you have but take for granted. I've said it before: The only reason the grass is greener on the other side is because someone is working to make it that way.

A joyful approach to life has a lot to do with nurturing a heart of gratitude. When we become truly thankful for what we have, our eyes are opened to the positives that we can celebrate and embrace. As we approach what is at hand from a heart that is willing to serve, to give, to love even when the going gets rough, God honors us by bringing change, increase, and promotion into our lives. Every sassy girl knows that it is only in being faithful in the little things that she can become ruler over much.

Check Yourself

- What is your present attitude toward your work? Your boss? Your husband? Those whom you serve?

- How can you transform your attitude into a more joyful one?

- What things should you be thankful for in your present position?

- How can you be a credit to the Lord in your place of employment?

- What should be your ultimate goal at work?

Personal Thoughts & Meditations

4 *Hospitality*

She is like the merchant ships,
bringing her food from afar.

Proverbs 31:14

ooking is one of many secret weapons in a woman's arsenal. They don't call it comfort food for nothing. It was after serving the king a meal that Esther was able to put her loving ruler in the mood to save her nation. Small wonder the enemy of our souls has sought to minimize the importance of cooking and the dinner table. Every woman knows the significance of a meal lovingly prepared by her hands and the importance of fellowshiping over a meal.

Fellowship breeds intimacy, which will reveal what we need to address. The dinner table is not just a place of sustenance; it is a place of comfort and safety. Jesus shared His heart with His disciples at the table. It's where He shared principles about the kingdom of God with those who were searching for redemption. Remember when families ate together at dinnertime? It was a better, safer world. Why? Because if something was wrong with your children or your spouse, it came out at the dinner table. It was noticed if someone's disposition seemed troubled or stressed, and the situation was usually addressed and put to rest. Now everyone goes separate ways and rarely is a meal shared. Not only has this made us a society of families sadly out of touch with one another, but we've become physically unhealthy as well.

In societies where meals are almost a ritual, where people take their time and savor every fresh course, folks are slimmer and in better physical condition. Why? Because they are eating in a relaxed state, which means they take the time to eat slowly, allowing their bodies to signal when they are full, as most nutritionalists will attest to. They eat smaller amounts of food that are properly digested because their bodies are not in a tense, on-the-go mode of being.

For some women cooking can be a daunting task. It doesn't have to be. Simple recipes are available in countless cookbooks, including my book *The Diva Principle.* Take the time to have fun and experiment until you've mastered a repertoire of meals. Once you've prepared a meal and experienced the appreciation of others enjoying what your hands have prepared, you will be inspired. When you prepare a meal for people, it makes them feel valued because you have taken the time to invest in them. You are imparting a piece of yourself to your guests. Small wonder Jesus compared Himself to the bread He served His disciples when He spoke to them of what they needed in order to have true life. Your presence and attention in the lives of others should be as filling, healing, and satisfying as the meal you serve. This is communion at its deepest level of exchange.

Check Yourself

- What is your attitude toward cooking?

- What are the things that hinder you from preparing meals for your family or friends?

- Which of the things you listed above can be rectified? How?

- In what ways can you make more time for nurturing others with a meal?

- When others enjoy what you prepare, how does it make you feel? What is the effect on them?

Personal Thoughts & Meditations

---

*I*n the olden days merchant ships caused major excitement when they came into port. Those on land knew that these vessels came loaded down with delights accumulated from their many travels. No one expected the same old fare. It was a time of great anticipation to see new things that would expand their palates as well as their knowledge of faraway places.

I recall dinner at my mother's house pretty much the same way. One night we would enjoy Mexican cuisine, another night Hawaiian, another evening West Indian, and some nights American. We never knew what she was serving up next, but we wanted to be there to experience it. I preferred to bring guests home for dinner versus eating at other people's houses because I so thoroughly enjoyed my mother's cooking. It was where I got a taste of the world before I ventured out to experience it geographically. It prepared me to be open to trying new things and becoming more world savvy.

On a high school trip to France I was one of very few in my group who ate well and enjoyed every bite of what was offered. The others refused to eat food foreign to them and spent most of their time hungry or looking for a McDonalds. Some were simply not ready for the world, and it affected their enjoyment of the trip dramatically.

Variety is the spice of life. This is evident in God's creation. Perhaps we avoid what we see as mundane tasks because of their sameness. How do we inject joy into our everyday musts? By flipping the script, by finding new dishes to experiment with. A new way to approach our regular rituals. Follow someone home and learn how they prepared that yummy dish you just tasted. Widen your repertoire and make the enjoyment of fellowshiping over a delicious meal contagious at your house. Be a haven to the weary, the thirsty, the hungry. The gift of hospitality is rare and treasured by all who get to partake of it.

Check Yourself

- Do you delight in variety?

- In what ways do you experiment with life?

- What rituals have you established in your day-to-day?

- What can you do to make the mundane exciting?

- How can your approach to these tasks be a blessing to others?

Personal Thoughts & Meditations

5 Starting Your Day

She gets up while it is still dark;
    she provides food for her family
and portions for her servant girls.

PROVERBS 31:15

Sassy

I don't know about you, but I love to sleep. Yet sleep can be a robber. I find that when I rise early the day rolls out before me like a fine carpet. And even more gets accomplished when I take the time to anchor my spirit first, to partake of spiritual bread along with my toast. It is really the habit of the diligent to rise early and set the day on course by first centering in the center of the One who created divine order.

Jesus rose early to get His marching orders and prepare His spirit for the day at hand. That's how He faced the world at large. Perhaps this is why the masses were unable to upset Him, to yank Him out of the Spirit, to pull Him down to their level of desperation. He was anchored in the trust He established during those early morning visits with His heavenly Father. Jesus used His morning time to set the course for the day. He was ahead of the game, not struggling to catch up. We are to live life proactively as opposed to defensively. This can only be accomplished as we place ourselves firmly in God's hands as we stand at the helm of the day.

Taking the time to be quiet, to hear Jesus' voice, to receive His instruction, and to locate your needs before the day begins is imperative to a healthy spiritual diet. This is where true sustenance begins—not with natural bread but with that which is served at a spiritual table. Eat lasting fare that nourishes your soul and fortifies your spirit.

Check Yourself

- Why is quiet time in the morning so important for setting your day in order?

- What happens when you don't take time to center your spirit before your day begins?

- What is the difference communing with God makes in your day?

- What distractions can rob you of this precious time? What can you do to be more consistent in this practice?

- In what ways can you nurture your spiritual diet daily?

Personal Thoughts & Meditations

*I*n instructions on how to respond during an emergency on a plane, people are instructed to first put the oxygen masks over their own faces before attempting to assist anyone else. This is very practical advice. Before you can help someone who is broken or seeking directon, you must be whole and grounded yourself. Jesus spent time in the Father's presence being refreshed. How much more do we, who are completely bogged down in our humanity, need to spend time being refueled to meet the challenges of the day-to-day!

God wants us to come into His presence consistently, not just for our own blessing but in order to fill us to overflowing so that we have a reservoir of abundant blessings to pour out on others. He longs to bless us so we might be blessings. He wants to grant us an excess of joy, peace, grace, and understanding that leaves us without an excuse for not helping others. Jesus, though He was a leader, was also a servant because of this extra reserve. He was able to minister to His disciples, His inner circle, and the masses without finding Himself on empty, tapped out from having to give entirely of Himself. As He fed on the bread of heaven, He was strengthened to feed others. This is where we struggle as women, as nurturers who take it upon ourselves to be all things to all people. From our family and loved ones to co-workers and our communities, many find themselves overextended trying to fill the endless needs. Only one Person can actually achieve such a lofty goal—Jesus. Our strength and supply for meeting the needs of others and feeding the hunger of their souls comes from our quiet time with the One who equips us for service to all He places in our path.

Check Yourself

- Do you have an overflow of spiritual food to offer others on a daily basis?

- What drains your energy? Your joy?

- What do you need to do to restore what has been depleted in your spirit?

- In what ways do you feel compelled to feed and nourish others?

- What must you do to prepare yourself to be a blessing to others?

Personal Thoughts & Meditations

Sowing & Reaping

She considers a field and buys it;
out of her earnings she
plants a vineyard.

PROVERBS 31:16 KJV

Consider where you invest your time, your giftings, your resources. Are they in the things that will yield a fruitful return? The choices you make today of where you sow your energy, attention, and all that has been entrusted into your care will have a profound effect on your tomorrows. God's Word encourages us to consider the cost before building (Luke 14:28). I would say this is true of every area of life, from relationships to material investments.

What you plant in the beginning of your associations will either bear the lush fruit of treasured friendship, deep abiding trust, honor, respect, lasting romance, and a legacy of wholeness in your children or dysfunctional relationships that neither bless you nor glorify God. We must consider the end of our actions or words as we meet and interact with others. First impressions are lasting ones. They set the course for the rest of the relationship...and even decide if the relationship will continue. Therefore, consider the seeds you plant carefully. You will harvest what you plant.

What about other areas of your life? Finances is always a good one to consider. Are you planting savings and investments that will bear the fruit of future security?

What about your health? This is another area where more thought should be given to the seeds we're planting. We are what we eat—spiritually as well as physically. What you ingest will manifest itself in good or bad health. Just a little food for thought: We will definitely reap what we sow!

Check Yourself

- What seeds are you planting to nurture rich fruit in your relationships?

- How are you sowing to reap a secure financial future?

- What seeds are you sowing to reap good health and soundness in your body?

- What weeds do you need to remove from your life?

- What good seeds have you planted? What bad seeds have you planted? What have you harvested from what you have sown?

- What would you like to plant more of in the future?

Personal Thoughts & Meditations

---

*G*od blesses us so we can, in turn, be a blessing to others. Sometimes being a blessing can cost us initially, yet this is the investment that must be made to yield an abundant crop for ourselves and for others. Jesus sowed His life in order to reap the lives of countless others who corporately make up the church, His bride. The ultimate sacrifice was made to gain the ultimate prize—the thing He loved most—us.

As we picture the life we want to live—what we would like to gain from our relationships and interactions, what we would like our hard work to yield—we must become cognizant of what is required to get what we want out of every area. What must be done to gain the life we want and the love we need? We must give our all. We must buy into the concept of investing ourselves fully in order to reap a rich return. If you are not a risk taker, I warn you now that love is not for the faint of heart. Whether in business or in love, anyone who has achieved his or her dream has a story to tell of losing it all. The Proverbs 31 woman made the initial investment of buying a field, which probably put her at a deficit initially. But as she reaped a return from that field, she accumulated the proceeds, turned them over and invested in something that would make money for her as she slept. She found something that would increase without her constant supervision. When you plant the right seeds you don't have to look longingly for your harvest to come. Increase will be a natural by-product of what you have sown. So sow carefully, sow deeply, and sow abundantly.

Check Yourself

- Are you considering how to best invest your gifts and resources?

- What are you willing to sacrifice in order to sow toward your future blessings?

- Do you take stock of what you are planting in the lives of others?

- In what areas do you need to increase sowing?

- How do you rate yourself in the area of financial responsibility?

- Write down what you want your harvest to look like spiritually, financially, emotionally, and socially. What will you sow in order to reap what you desire?

Personal Thoughts & Meditations

7 Using Your Gifts

She sets about her work vigorously;
her arms are strong for her tasks.
She sees that her trading is profitable,
and her lamp does
not go out at night.

I've said it countless times: Attitude is everything. What does that mean when it comes to the way that we approach our work? It's simple. If we love what we are doing, we will do it in excellence. If we don't, we will not put forth the effort to be and do our best. I've been guilty of this myself. I confess that when I no longer liked my job it manifested in ways that were not profitable to the company I worked for or myself. For instance, I was constantly late. Why? Because I wasn't looking forward to being there. Every distraction was a welcome one when I was getting ready in the morning. My service was poor because I didn't care; I didn't care about the customer or my boss or the company I worked for. And believe me, my attitude showed. It showed so much that I was eventually fired. My lack of interest led me to not paying attention and missing important details that eventually landed me in a heap of trouble when I botched a project badly. It ended up costing our client a lot of money to redo it properly. The fallout was embarrassing.

Not only was my job affected, my physical well-being was as well. To counter my boredom during the day I got caught up in a cycle of distractions after work that went late into the night. So you know what happened, right? I was too tired to get up the next morning to go to work. I suffered from fatigue on top of my boredom and bad attitude. Well after a while not only did my work suffer, my health did too. One feeds the other. Bad health and poor focus equals even worse attitude and sloppy work. Get the picture?

If truly we are doing our work as unto the Lord, we prepare ourselves to be excellent every day by taking care of ourselves physically and emotionally. Be honest with yourself. Should you be doing the work you're doing or should you find something that your gifts complement and you personally enjoy? Then make sure you get the rest and exercise you need, along with a proper diet, so that you function at peak performance. It's not just about how you feel and look at work. Remember that you represent God. And for that reason alone you should always put your best foot…as well as your best work…forward.

Check Yourself

- How do you apply yourself to your work? Are you up to your tasks?

- What is your attitude toward customer service?

- What elements contribute to you being physically exhausted? How does exhaustion affect your work? How do you operate when you are at your physical peak?

- If you were an employer, what would you want and expect from your workers? Are you delivering what you would want?

• What do you need to do to be a worker who brings honor
  to God and blessings to others?

Personal Thoughts & Meditations

———————

*P*art of enjoying your work is knowing that what you have to
offer others is good and needed. Knowing that you have contributed
something to the betterment of others is a fulfilling feeling. This
can be tenuous if you are dealing with low self-esteem issues. Take
note: *You are a rare gift to the world.* God made you on purpose
with certain built-in giftings to serve others. He saw these as good
things. The problem is that most of us don't know what our gifts
are, which leads us to take jobs and pursue professions that leave
us wanting more.

But when you locate your gifts and learn how to apply them
in a way that will profit you and bless others, you live at the peak
of joy and fulfillment. This will only occur when you realize that
the abilities you have and take for granted are the very thing that
someone else wishes he or she could do! That is why they are called
gifts. Realize that what you have to offer is a good thing—a good
thing to be shared with others. Now what are you going to do about

it? How are you going to parlay those gifts into a profitable life for yourself as well as others?

Start today to do an assessment of what you have to offer. Think about what others seek from you and the effect you have on others when you use your gifts in ways that bless them. Think about how it makes God smile when you utilize all that He has placed within you. These are the things that make you feel as if you are living your best life no matter how much money you are making or not making. This is when you discover it is not material gain that gives joy; it is the embracing of the very purpose for which you were created—using your gifts to the fullest capacity possible for God's glory.

Check Yourself

- How do you perceive the worth of your gifts? Of your work?

- What is your main gift? How can that ability be used to bless others? To be profitable for yourself?

- In what ways do you get to use your gift at the job you presently have?

- Why is your job a gift? What things have you been taking for granted about your job? What attitudes need to shift for you to once again be joyful about your work?

- In what way does your work contribute to the betterment of your employer? Of your family? Of your community?

Personal Thoughts & Meditations

———————

There is a big difference between doing just enough and going the extra mile. The difference is whether you will excel or not. As quiet as it's kept, most of the world is living below its greatest potential. The business of service is suffering. It is every man and woman for themselves. The average salaried employee is doing just enough to get his check. If you want to know the difference between those who live the average life and those who excel, simply look at people's work habits. Those who excel operate on little sleep. They are up early and go to bed late. So driven are they by their vision that they think and do little else. They are consumed by their passion to serve, produce, and contribute to the world! These are the happiest people because their lives are driven by their sense of purpose. This is not reliance on the responses of others for affirmation. They answer to a higher call.

Your lamp not going out is not about staying up all night and burning the candle at both ends. It's about generating the type of excitement and love for your work that has you always moving forward—even when you're sleeping. You anticipate new ideas and ways to improve your current service. Coming up with ways to make money while you sleep, as some would say. But this comes from being *totally* invested in what you are doing. First, you sense that others need what you have to offer. Second, you derive great joy from meeting the needs of others and getting the chance to serve while doing what you love to do. Third, you are cognizant of the fact that you are glorifying God through your work expression. These things become fuel to your mind, spirit, and body, and they energize you and give you more zest for life. Gone is the fatigue that plagues many who are not enjoying what they do. For those who love what they do, their lamps never go out!

Check Yourself

- How would you describe your work ethic?

- How diligent are you to complete your tasks?

- What energizes you about what you do?

- What do you look forward to most about your work?

- In what ways can you nurture more enthusiasm on a daily basis for what you do? How can this new attitude be a blessing to others? To yourself?

Personal Thoughts & Meditations

Giving

In her hand she holds the distaff and grasps the spindle with her fingers. She opens her arms to the poor and extends her hands to the needy.

PROVERBS 31:20

Sassy

The Scripture says that the hands of the virtuous woman were busy spinning thread and twisting fibers. This gave me pause when I considered the verse that says the foolish woman tears down her house with her own hands. I thought of the damage we do with our hands in the spiritual sense. "Don't get it twisted" is a popular phrase, yet our words and our perspective can slant things in such a way that others are hurt. Though we may not be "spinning" in the sense of fabrication, we do spin things by what we stir up with our words and actions.

Women are creative. We see the invisible, hear the inaudible, and feel the intangible. But we must be careful that we are not seeing, hearing, and feeling the wrong things or reacting to our slanted perceptions. Let's not be busy just for busy's sake and create the wrong things. Let's put our hands to good work creating things and situations that bring life and joy to others, that empower others to be their best. Let's put our hands to work that will last and add to the lives of others.

As you reflect on your everyday interactions and conversations, be cognizant of the things you "spin." As you listen to others or experience different encounters, pay attention to whether you view those moments through a distorted lens because of your own unresolved issues. Remember, in order to be a blessing to others we must first unravel our own past issues and free our hearts from anything that might have them bound and unable to reach out to others. Decide not to empower those who affect you negatively by giving in to bad moods and wrong attitudes. Instead, spin a new scenario that is positive and life-giving for yourself, as well as to those around you who need it. Whatever you spin, positive or negative, someone is sure to "wear" it.

Check Yourself

- What reactions or results do your words often create?

- What types of things have you had a wrong perception of in the past? What was your reaction? What was the result?

- In what areas must you be careful to think before reacting?

- What happens when you perceive something in the wrong way? How can you safeguard against this in the future?

- Consider what your words and actions create in the lives of others. If they were garments, what would you like to see others wearing?

Personal Thoughts & Meditations

_I_ n recent years we've seen a movement of celebrities reaching out to the poor in many nations. The move is on to end poverty! And yet Jesus said we would have the poor with us always. On the flip side of that, we are told that we are our brother's keeper, and what we do to the least of people we also do to Christ. It is impressive to see these famous icons remembering to give back, being driven by a greater passion than fame—that of a need to help the hungry and the dying. But what about those who don't have vast resources? Jesus seemed to be more impressed by those who had little but were still driven to give. That screamed volumes more to Him than those who were generous because they already had a lot. The truly generous man or woman is the one who doesn't have a lot but chooses to give anyway out of what he or she has. Generous people sacrifice so that someone else can have. This is what Jesus did for us. He gave until it hurt.

Fact: God blesses us so we may be blessings to others. This defies the present law of consumption that many of us walk in accordance with. But real giving reaches beyond our overflow into our private stores. It is the place where our best resources are, where we are forced to give the gift of ourselves. And this can be really scary—but even more rewarding. And the saying is still true: It is more blessed to give than to receive.

Check Yourself

- Are you compelled to serve others who are less fortunate than yourself? To what degree?

- How easy is it for you to embrace others who are not like yourself?

- What things scare you or keep you from giving more to the less fortunate?

- How do you feel when you've blessed people with something they need?

- What can you purpose to do on a regular basis to help those in need?

Personal Thoughts & Meditations

───────

I find it interesting that the virtuous woman in Proverbs 31 extended her arms to the poor and her hands to the needy. Obviously she perceived a difference between the two. The poor suffered from material lack while the needy suffered from emotional or spiritual needs. How quick we are to distance ourselves from those who are not like us. And yet this woman in Proverbs who had plenty extended her *arms* to the poor. She embraced them. She didn't merely toss a few shekels their way. She stopped to interact with them, to carefully consider their plight. She pulled them in close and listened to their heartbeats. This is the only way we can effectively minister to the disenfranchised, to the homeless, to the poor, to those who have seemingly insurmountable needs. Perhaps their true needs are neither apparent nor suitable for a quick fix. Far too many times our consciences are soothed by throwing monetary solutions to those who need much more. They long for restoration and a chance at dignity.

Recently one of my cohosts of the television show *Aspiring Women* took on the challenge of spending a night with the homeless. She was deeply affected by what she found: Men and women who were homeless because of circumstances that many of us would never have considered. Moved to tears, she said she would never judge those she saw begging on the street again. Based on what she learned as she spoke heart-to-heart with those she met, she concluded most of America was one paycheck away from being homeless. It was a sobering and eye-opening experience.

The needy are different from the poor. The circumstances of life, shattered dreams, broken relationships, dashed expectations, rejections—these can take a toll on the human heart, leaving it scarred, wounded, and in search of mending and reassurance. A hands-on approach is needed. Sometimes a touch can do more than anything we could say or give. Truly being present with those who need our ears, our guidance, and perhaps even our participation in their mending is called for. We are to mourn with those who mourn and weep with those who weep. Helping the needy, like helping the poor, calls for investing our whole selves. The difference is knowing when to release the needy to soar on their own so they don't remain needy and refuse the restoration that ultimately only God can give. We are merely vessels of His caring. We're reflections of His love as we make ourselves available to those who need us most. This becomes our greatest blessing as we see the rewards of our handiwork before us.

Check Yourself

- How sensitive are you to the needs of others?

- Are you aware of how to adjust your approach or touch when dealing with others' needs?

- What is your first inclination when encountering someone who has a financial need? Why?

- In what ways can you reach out to those in need?

- When you've helped someone less fortunate than yourself or someone in need, how do you feel as you see your contribution making a difference?

Personal Thoughts & Meditations

Persevering

When it snows,
    she has no fear for her household;
for all of them are clothed in scarlet.

PROVERBS 31:21

I have taught myself to say in the midst of good times or bad, "This too shall pass." Inevitably it will, and we must be prepared. To be able to laugh at the snow when it arrives speaks volumes about our ability to plan for times that might not be so comfortable. Preparing for adverse conditions does not imply a lack of faith. It suggests that we have a sound understanding of the signs of the times and the knowledge that even the righteous are not exempt from hardship. It rains on the just and the unjust (Matthew 5:45). God simply gives those who know Him the grace and strength to endure and flourish in spite of the elements.

In Proverbs it tells us that even the ants prepare for the winter. I believe that many of us live in denial that there will be times that are not of the ease we would like. Yet if we understand that life will have times of sun, snow, and rain, we will prepare ourselves accordingly and weather each one well. Winter represents the time when there is no harvest. It is the time when the earth lies barren with no fruit in sight. But harvest precedes winter. Therefore, if you reap well and store your goods well you can rest secure when the cold sets in. You too can laugh when you seemingly are threatened by lack.

I'm not talking about just physical lack. Yes, you should make sure you have money saved for a rainy day. But you should also be spiritually fortified. Your faith should be well anchored *before* you need it. You should know that Jesus is *Jehovah Jireh* before you need a financial blessing. Be steadfastly sure in your faith so that when the storm hits you still stand secure, unshakeable, immoveable, not bowed over by fear because you know in whom you have placed your trust. You are not reliant on physical bread for your strength. You've stored God's Word in your heart. You have bread from heaven to feed you in times of famine. Because of the One who feeds you, you have health and strength. Not only do you have enough for yourself, you have a reserve to feed others. Being anchored in God makes you a haven for others to cling to during the hard times. And that is truly something to celebrate!

Check Yourself

- How sensitive are you to the seasons of your life?

- In what ways do you anticipate the future and prepare for it?

- What season of life are you in? What things are needed to weather this season well?

- What do you see coming in your life? How will you prepare?

- How will you balance your present season with transitioning into the next?

Personal Thoughts & Meditations

E verything must change. To some that is a scary thought. I don't know about you, but when I get in a groove I crawl in with both feet and am content for things to stay exactly as they are. This is about the time God decides to mix things up a bit by introducing a new melody to my song. Even though it's catchy, it takes me a moment to adjust and welcome the change. We are creatures of comfort. Though we say we like variety, there is an unspoken comfort in consistency that we tend to embrace.

God knows that change is necessary because change equals growth. And so He begins by allowing us to grow uncomfortable where we are or to grow weary of a circumstance. For those who have a hard time catching a clue, He can allow the situation we are deeply entrenched in to become absolutely unbearable. By the time He introduces our new option, we are more than ready to go.

Yes, sometimes God has to shake us up to get us moving. Just as we long to be blessed, He longs to bless us. Sometimes we must grow into our blessings, and God is determined to keep us on track for the blessings He so passionately wants to bestow. So grow we must; change we must. It is the cycle of life. Everything about the order of God reveals this. The opposite of growth and change is stagnancy. Not good. Whatever is not growing is dying. So though sometimes growing pains accompany transition, embrace them. They will show you the things you need to shed and the things you need to add. They will show you the path to maturity and strength. And at the end of the day, when you've come through to the other side, yes, you will laugh.

Check Yourself

- How well do you adapt to change?

- What do you resist most about change?

- What scares you the most?

- How important is being in control to you?

- What have you learned about God in the times you let go and yielded to the change? How can your faith be built from this experience to face change in the future?

Personal Thoughts & Meditations

*C*onfidence in the Lord is essential to everyday living. Inevitably all the other things we trust in will fail us. People, material possessions, you name it. At some point in time human resources run out, and we are left to fall on the grace of God once again. God forewarned the Israelite nation that if they turned to Egypt in the midst of their difficulties they would fall down together. The blind leading the blind will never arrive at their desired destination. Only God can clearly see the solution in the midst of darkness. Only He can chart a steady course through confusion. Only He can restore plenty in the deepest valley of lack. Small wonder God allows us to come to the end of ourselves time and time again until we can get this one right.

I recall spending a year in California that stripped me of all I knew until I came face-to-face with Jehovah Jireh, my Provider. It was in the place of the greatest lack I had ever known that I came to learn firsthand about the provision of God. His ability to make a way out of no way could not be denied by the end of my excruciating year. Much to the chagrin of my pride, I came to the end of myself and all of my own resourcefulness. That's when God showed up and revealed who was really taking care of me. This encounter with a benevolent provider cemented in my spirit forever that God would take care of me. In the face of my own helplessness and yes, even sometimes in spite of my poor choices and decisions, my Abba Father covered me and supplied my needs according to His promises. As time went by, my trust in God grew in the area of His care. After all, I had experienced His goodness and knew He was faithful. No one could take that knowledge from me. It is only after we've been tried that God proves Himself best and reveals the true source of confidence.

Check Yourself

- How do you deal with situations that are out of your control?

- Do you walk in fear or faith when things occur that are beyond your power to fix? Why?

- What does your response say about your relationship with God?

- What is your first response to unexpected circumstances?

- In what ways do you need to renew your mind so you can turn to God first? How will this alter your response?

Personal Thoughts & Meditations

10

Discretion

She makes coverings for her bed;
she is clothed in fine
linen and purple.

PROVERBS 31:22

Sassy

$\mathcal{I}$ 've got you covered." These are reassuring words when uttered by those we trust. Discretion is something that most must learn, yet it is essential to the preservation of any relationship we prize. From marriage to close friendships, covering the things that matter most to the one you love is a sure way to build intimacy. Secrets bind us together. And trials endured, shared, and kept in confidence become the cement of a solid foundation for all that we exchange over time.

The greatest violation of a relationship is that of uncovering a loved one, making him or her vulnerable to the attack and ridicule of others. Noah's son Ham was cursed for not covering his father and instead, exposing him to humiliation (Genesis 9:22-25). We are also told that a matter repeated separates friends. God Himself covers our sins and casts them into the sea of forgetfulness never to discuss them again.

Discretion is listed as one of the traits of wisdom in Proverbs 9 and one of the ingredients of a woman's life that leads to riches, honor, and a long life (see verse 19). Truly riches cannot be measured just materially. Our relationships can cause us to feel wealthier than the biggest magnate if they are rich in exchange, confidences, love, and support. The Proverbs 31 woman not only covered her bed with fine linens, she covered it with intimacy between her and her husband. The things they shared in this place that was their inner sanctuary, the secrets whispered on their pillows, remained there, kept between them like breaths exchanged—experienced but not seen.

The invisible tie that binds begins when two begin to speak the language of one and understanding comes in a glance without words because of what has already been spoken in the secret place. The same can be said of friends who have laughed, cried, and hurt together, who have borne each other's greatest dreams and deepest disappointments without gossiping. Loyalty is built and sustained on this trust. "I've got you covered" are words of consolation, words of intimacy.

Check Yourself

- How protective are you of others' personal affairs?

- Do your husband, friends, and loved ones trust you with their secrets?

- In what ways do you exercise discretion in your personal interactions?

- Why is discretion important in relationships?

- How can violating confidences be detrimental to a relationship? How does keeping confidences build intimacy?

Personal Thoughts & Meditations

———————————

_E_veryone must have a place of intimacy. A hidden sanctuary away from the eyes and ears of those who do not live at the heart of your relationship. For a husband and wife the bedroom is transformed into the garden of Eden once again. Naked and unashamed there is no need for them to remain covered as they stand open and vulnerable to one another. They become one another's best-kept secret. It is in this atmosphere that passion and romance is birthed and manifested. This is why it is so important to keep the sanctity of this very special place free from all that would distract or interfere.

Many who teach on how to keep romance alive talk about setting the atmosphere. Keep the bedroom free of television and other things that would distract the attention and focus of the couple to anything or anyone other than one another. Have candles, music, and scents that promote an atmosphere for sharing passion. Be intentional when it comes to keeping the home fires burning. There must be a place that is off limits to everyone else but you and your mate. This becomes your special "secret garden" where you can exchange what is most precious between you—yourselves. It is in this environment that a couple experiences the delight of being conspiratorial friends and lovers, enriching their relationship in a way that takes their love for one another to a new level of intimacy.

When sharing quality time with friends you cover them by creating an oasis for uninhibited conversation. A safe place to share from hearts freely without fear of reprisal or betrayal. Creating an atmosphere of comfort and trust is crucial for getting to the heart of friendship. Laughing with those who laugh, weeping with those who weep, being empathetic—feeling what those who confide in you share. People are in search of true confidantes where they can hide their hearts and release their pain and simply be themselves. As Christ is that for us, we must be that for others.

Check Yourself

- What components create a sanctuary environment for friends and loved ones? How do you create this?

- Where is the place you've set aside to make others feel covered and safe?

- How do you set the atmosphere for intimacy with your mate? With your friends?

- How do you set boundaries to protect the place of intimacy in your relationships?

- Why is a safe place important for nurturing intimacy?

Personal Thoughts & Meditations

---

*T*he best way to cover others is to first cover yourself: Cover yourself in prayer. Cover yourself with the perfume of the fruit of the Spirit. This comes from creating a sanctuary for you and God to visit, a place set apart to cultivate intimacy and allow His presence to uncover deep revelations that bring transformation into your life on a daily basis. This type of transformation becomes contagious to those around you.

In this secret place that belongs to you and the Lover of your soul alone, you are able to pour yourself out and gain clarity for your own life as well as for others. The still, small voice of God beckons us here, to a place set apart and purposefully selected for the sole agenda of meeting with Him. Again this is intentional; this is no haphazard meeting. You both anticipate the appointment.

This is a sweet time, a cleansing time, a refreshing time. And it shows when you don't enter into this place just as much as it does when you do. This meeting should become a personal ritual you can't do without. It is a necessity of the soul that feeds and revitalizes you, giving you the strength you need to be a blessing to others. You pick the time and the place to steal away, but steal away you must.

I confess that the bathtub used to be my special place. I had the best conversations with God there, but now I spend time with God in my living room. I'm all curled up on my ratchet couch early in the morning with my puppy snuggled at my feet. In the stillness I feel God's presence, and His goodness becomes overwhelming. He meets me here and whispers things to my spirit that I receive and carry. His promises, sometimes His warnings, but always His encouragement carries me through my day, giving me all I need to face every situation and every person who might need a fresh measure of grace to carry them through his or her day. This process is preparing yourself. And in those instances when you come face-to-face with challenges, you will hear a voice behind you saying, "Don't worry! I've got you covered."

Check Yourself

- How do you cover yourself? What boundaries do you set to guard your heart? The hearts of your loved ones?

- How do you create an atmosphere for communing with God?

- Why is the environment so important for intimate fellowship? What does the wrong environment do?

- What do you need to put into place to guard yourself from distractions?

- How does discipline factor in to protecting the atmosphere for prayer and worship?

Personal Thoughts & Meditations

11

Gift of Influence

*Her husband is respected
at the city gate,
where he takes his seat
among the elders of the land.*

<small>PROVERBS 31:23</small>

have to begin with the singles on this one, and then I'll move on to the married ladies. Women, how you begin will determine how you end and if you'll be able to say what this scripture conveys about your husband. Of course this will be a reflection of two choices you make. One—the caliber of the man you decide to marry, and two—the woman you choose to be in your marriage. Both of these decisions will determine the quality of man you end up living the rest of your life with.

In order for you to be the woman God has called you to be in marriage, you must carefully select to whom you say "I do." You should know the character of the man before you marry him. Is he a man you can respect and submit to? Is his character upstanding and honored among his peers? Getting married will not change the man. It will only intensify and manifest what is already hidden in his inner man. In other words, your presence in his life will help bring out the best or the worst in him.

Your influence in your man's life can, however, inspire him to be transformed as you live your life before him. Let me be clear on this so you don't think I'm contradicting myself. The Bible is clear that a woman's influence on a man is profound, but it will only highlight what is already in that man. This means a decent man can lurk behind a mean, surly guy who just needs consistent gentleness to let him know it's safe for him to be vulnerable. On the other hand, signs of disturbing character will always reveal itself if you wait long enough for that nice guy you're considering to be placed in a situation where pressure is applied. Don't ignore the signs, and don't fool yourself into thinking you are the one who can change anyone. Only the Holy Spirit can do so! And that still takes a person who is willing to surrender who he is in exchange for what God wants him to be. With this in mind, remember that you are not called to be God in your relationship; you are called to be a wife. So when selecting the man you plan to spend forever with, make sure he is a man you can celebrate and follow forever.

Check Yourself

- What type of men do you consistently attract?

- What type of man do you find attractive? How does this line up with who you attract?

- What benchmarks of character make you respect and honor the man in your life? What types of things make you reluctant to honor his leadership?

- In what ways have you been a positive influence in the lives of men who have been in your life?

- What types of things can you do to influence transformation in your man's life?

Personal Thoughts & Meditations

*O*kay married ladies, it's your turn. I once heard a great preacher say that if you don't like the man your husband has become you must reflect on your contribution to his character since you are his helpmeet. Ouch! What an awesome responsibility you have. God has given you the incredible gift of influence which, when wielded in the right hands, can be far more powerful than authority. No need for nagging and demanding. Just live as the woman God has created and called you to be! The Word tells us in 1 Peter 3:1, "Wives, in the same way be submissive to your husbands so that, if any of them do not believe the word, they may be won over without words by the behavior of their wives."

As you walk in a manner that honors God and your husband, not only will your mate be challenged to grow up into all that God has called him to, he will also be secure enough to release you to do the things God has placed on your life. Your partner will celebrate your giftings and the expressions of them if he feels that he is still your first priority (after God) in your life.

Generally when a man feels threatened he digs in his heels and seeks to control and oppress his woman. He will fight for power on one level or the other; therefore, it is crucial that a woman understand her ability to make her man feel emasculated or empowered. How he feels affects his character in the home and in the workplace. His ability to function in excellence in his work environment is also connected to his home life.

You get to help set the pace of his life by aligning his spirit, mind, and heart in a home where peace reigns. A man at peace with his God, his wife, and his family walks in integrity and excels. His character is such that it attracts honor and respect. He is celebrated by his peers and promoted in the marketplace. This is the legacy that can, in part, be attributed to a wife who walks in wisdom. Of course there are some exceptions to this rule, as in the testimony of Abigail found in 1 Samuel chapter 25, but even her story had a happy ending because she didn't allow the foolishness of her husband to dilute who she was. The bottom line? Be the woman you were created to be and the wife that your man needs, and you will be sure to see the good fruit of your labor.

Check Yourself

- How do you contribute to the greatness of the man in your life?

- Are you an exhorter? In what ways do you feed him confidence?

- How quick or slow are you to praise him for things he does well? How critical are you?

- How do you provoke him to good works? How involved are you in feeding your man in the area of his dreams? In what ways?

- Does he feel he contributes anything to your world that garners your respect and adoration? How does this empower him to release you to your own pursuits?

Personal Thoughts & Meditations

_____

This whole "making a man feel like a man" brings up the entire issue of submission. You know, that one word that no matter how holy we might be we end up gritting our teeth at the thought of? Mm hmm. I feel your pain. Hopefully I can liberate you from it in the light of sharing some understanding.

Say slowly and to yourself: "Submission is not about being a doormat; it is about putting myself in the position to be blessed." It is also an act of love in marriage. It is giving the one you love the gift of being a valuable contributor to your life. As we submit to God, we are blessed. The more we submit, the more blessed we become. There are blessings God gives us out of His unconditional love for us, but there are also blessings with conditions attached to them. As we cooperate with His will, He is delighted to entrust us with more and more blessings as we prove ourselves trustworthy. The same holds true for our mates. (If you're single, this applies to the ones in authority over you, such as a boss. As we become team players we yield to the one who has the responsibility of directing and covering us.)

In a marriage arena this responsibility shifts between the two of you, depending on what is needed in order to get the job done. A couple that is truly biblical is submitted to one another. They recognize one another's strengths and yield leadership to each other depending on the other's giftings. But even in the context of a husband handing over something of great portent to the woman, he does not feel as if his headship role is threatened by her leadership. I've spoken about this in one of my other books, *The Diva Principle,* in reference to Deborah who was a judge over Israel but still a wife. She had mastered the balance of being a leader and a woman with an amazing grace that still allowed the men who surrounded her to rise up to the occasion and fight and lead when they were needed to do so. This balance can take some time to master, but when it comes to maturity in a woman the results can be absolutely incredible. Remember: True power lies in empowering others.

Check Yourself

- What is your attitude toward submission?

- Where have you encountered problems with submission in the past? What was the outcome of your resistance?

- In what areas do you find yourself resistant to instruction or cooperation with your husband? Your boss? Those in authority over you?

- What is the underlying issue or fear related to you submitting? What do you feel you will lose if you yield?

- What do you stand to gain if you can master the art of submission in your life? From God? In your home? In your workplace? With friends and associates?

Personal Thoughts & Meditations

12

Success

She makes linen garments and sells them, and supplies the merchants with sashes.

PROVERBS 31:24

Your God-given gifts are not just gifts to you. According to God's design, they are gifts to others as well. Balancing what should be given away and what will be appreciated if it is a premium can become a sticky issue for most who simply want to bless people. However, in God's economy He has dispensed gifts for different purposes. One is to equip others personally, emotionally, and spiritually. Others were designed to actually prosper the giver of the gift. This was something I wrestled with for years until I had an epiphany one day.

At a time when I was struggling financially I was bemoaning my fate to the Lord. He spoke to me and said, "It is not my fault that you do not have money, Michelle. I have equipped you with gifts to prosper you, and you keep giving them away for free." Well, you could have knocked me over with a feather! I thought I was being a nice little Christian by volunteering for everything and using my writing abilities to bless others for free. Every time someone needed something written I volunteered and gladly did it without financial compensation. Writing came easily to me, and it almost seemed like a crime to charge people for something that was like child's play to me. And yet it was God's gift to me for the purpose of provision. This was a new revelation for me, and it was also the birth of my new business as a freelance writer. As I began to put value to the gifts God had given me, I began to attract clients and increase my business and the sphere of my gifts.

A woman I recently interviewed on the show I cohost (*Aspiring Women*) loved to make pies. People were always asking her to bake a pie for them for one occasion or another. This gave way to a booming business—you guessed it, a pie shop! Gifts that were once taken for granted can be bigger blessings as we apply ourselves to serving others but also to being wise stewards of the gifts for God's sake as well as our own. Little becomes much as we partner with God to grow the seed.

Check Yourself

- What natural gifts do you have that can be utilized to bless others and prosper yourself?

- In what ways can your giftings serve as a covering for others?

- How do your gifts add to the life of others?

- In what ways do you prosper as a person as you share your gifts with others? Financially? Emotionally? Spiritually?

- How do your abilities grow as you share your gifts with others?

Personal Thoughts & Meditations

---

*W*hen examining the principle of increase in the area of our gifts, we must make sure our motivation is to serve. The Proverbs 31 woman made linen garments to sell. This was a needed article. She was in tune with the season and the needs of those around her. The most successful businesses are those that locate the needs of people and seek to fill that need. Linen was the order of the day for the region she lived in because it was a cool fabric that would breathe in the arid conditions. This was what most people wore in order to move easily about their day. Tunics that covered but did not cling were functional garments that were needed by most. Her choice of enterprise was not a whimsical one; it was based on the needs of those around her. Consequently, her business was profitable.

The secret is finding something people need but cannot or will not supply for themselves. I love to buy gifts for people that I know they would love but would never purchase. It is an indulgence they put off for another time but usually never get around to because it is a want versus a need. But in some cases their need is something they simply don't know how to fill. That's where you come in. I believe God has given each one of us something that works in a unique fashion to address the needs of someone who does not have the time or means to get what he or she needs without your help. In the giving of yourself, as well as your gifts, in essence you cover others. They are no longer vulnerable to an element of need because you have filled it. Whether that is something as simple as the need for nourishment or some other sort of service, the individuals receiving from you are more complete than they were before they were blessed by you and what you had to offer. Not only are they the better for the encounter and exchange, but your life is enriched just knowing that at the end of the day you made a positive difference in the lives of people who were able to celebrate and appreciate what you imparted to them. This is a major key to being a reflection of God's care and provision.

Check Yourself

- What do you have that others need?

- How does filling the needs of others fill the need in you?

- What would you do for free if money weren't an issue in your life?

- How can you begin to do that now to serve others?

- In what ways can this become profitable to you?

Personal Thoughts & Meditations

---

ake note! Our sassy Proverbs 31 diva wasn't simply a merchandiser and tradesperson—she was also a wholesaler. She supplied sashes or belts to the merchants for resale. She was a trendsetter, an innovator, a suppler to suppliers! God gives seed to the sower. This merely means He empowers us and supplies us with what we need to plant and reap a productive harvest in our lives. The Proverbs 31 woman imitated this principle. I think there are two ways we can look at this. First, she was a supplier to suppliers. We all have the capacity to do this to some extent with those in our lives. She empowered others to profit by what she furnished them with. We can do the same thing for others materially, spiritually, and emotionally.

Perhaps people need courage, good advice, or physical help to achieve something that would make them a blessing to others, and this would also cause them to reap the fruit of sound relationships or an increase in business. You may be able to furnish not just the physical resources but the wisdom and the connections—whatever is needed to help people make it to where they want to go. Perhaps you are the master of great networking. That is a huge skill to be able to direct people to the right resources and opportunities. I think of those who have stepped in and introduced me to this person or that person, who were then able to open huge doors to a profitable end. Being one who supplies either the things needed or the route to get to success takes your gift of resourcefulness to another level.

Second, I would say the Proverbs 31 woman sold more than she bought. This is a major key to financial empowerment. She turned the tables on consumerism! She supplied to the merchants! Think of what you have that can be marketed for the betterment of others. From material items to sage advice, you should reap more input than output. This goes back to the theory of coming up with inventions that afford you the luxury of making money while you sleep…of marketing your gifts not only to bless others but to prosper yourself. There should be increase attached to all you offer. This increase can be material, spiritual, or emotional. If it is not something with residual effect, then the return should be immediate gain of some sort. The bottom line is it should not cost you anything you are not willing to sacrifice to be a blessing! Remember that the blessings of the Lord makes rich and adds no sorrow (Proverbs 10:22). So be a blessing and be blessed.

Check Yourself

- What do you have to offer others that can add to the their lives?

- Which of your activities are draining and not conducive to fruitfulness? In what ways?

- What relationships and activities are fruitful? In what ways?

- What must you do to make sure your output provides significant returns?

- Who are the merchants in your life, and what supplies will you give them?

Personal Thoughts & Meditations

13 *Resilience*

She is clothed
with strength and dignity;
she can laugh at the days to come.

PROVERBS 31:25

There is a sweetness that comes from weathering trials that a person who has never suffered or persevered through difficulties and disappointments will never be able to manifest. It is the ointment that is squeezed from the petals of roses and other precious flowers that makes a priceless perfume called Joy. So it is with us that as life squeezes us what is within is manifested for all to see either in the form of a grace that glorifies God or a rage that confirms that our flesh is still very much the dominant force in our lives.

Trials will either make us bitter or better, and the choice is up to us. We can choose to squeeze our pain—embrace it like a friend and allow it to teach us lessons that make us better for the experience. Or we can choose to flail at the world and our circumstances, never owning the piece in the situation that belongs to us. If we are not alert observers we become blind participants in a drama that was never meant to entertain. It was meant to reveal something about our nature, something about an area overlooked or ignored that we need to address to become more of what God has designed us to be. The Word tells us, "No discipline seems pleasant at the time....Later on, however, it produces a harvest of righteousness and peace" (Hebrews 12:11). This is fruit that remains. Others enjoy its scent and its offerings because it is sweet.

You've met them—people who drew you to them though they

never said a word. There was something so special about them—a kindness, a gentility, an empathy that you didn't sense in others. And as you drew close and engaged in deep conversation with them, you learned of the things they had endured in their lives. You shook your head, wondering how they could survive such pain and bounce back time and time again. How could they endure and recover? Forgive again and again? You were drawn to them. And, yes, you even longed to hold them and telegraph your sympathy and understanding. They were so…sweet.

And yet there was a resilience about them that garnered your respect. A quiet strength that didn't shout or demand attention. It simply was, and you thought to yourself, *I want to be like that when I grow up.* All I can say is consider the price of that strength. And if you've found it too high, ask for the grace to pay it and allow God to perfect you.

Check Yourself

- Have the affairs of life and love made you better or bitter? In what ways?

- What things have the pain you've suffered told you about yourself?

- What truths do you need to address? In what ways?

- How can your trials make you stronger?

- How can others be blessed by the things you've endured?

Personal Thoughts & Meditations

$\mathcal{S}$he took it like a lady" is a phrase one doesn't hear that often anymore. Recently I was watching a program where two women had a public disagreement. In the interest of preserving her pride, one lady made a move to preserve herself that left the other lady feeling betrayed and powerless. Her comment was, "We were hoping that she would handle the situation with more dignity." Depending on your definition of dignity, you might have thought she did, while another clearly felt she had not. True dignity cannot be disputed.

True dignity rises above the fray to walk on its own level above faultfinding and the preservation of pride. It takes the high road that is not often used. It does not seek to secure its position but leaves that to God and those who will be silenced by its pursuit of peace.

Dignity walked the Via Dolorosa in Jerusalem under a cumbersome cross because He knew who He was though others failed to recognize Him. Christ was the epitome of dignity. He did not insist on His own way. Neither did He demand of anyone, "Do you know who I am?" He walked through the fray of the insecurity and hatred of others. Or, more to the point, He transcended the fray without being moved from who He was. He remained gracious, loving, and even compassionate toward those who had none of that to give Him.

I believe that dignity is birthed from knowing and understanding that your identity is hidden in the One who cannot be changed or moved from His position concerning you—God Himself. No matter what anyone else says or does, your value remains intact. As you walk in this understanding, there is no circumstance or reaction that can move you from who you are or squeeze anything distasteful out of you. You consistently live with graciousness and dignity.

Check Yourself

- How do you respond when your pride or position is challenged?

- In what ways are you tempted to fight back when you feel wronged by someone? What is usually the outcome of this course of action?

- What do you believe about yourself when others pit themselves against you?

- In what ways can you cultivate a greater sense of identity that is not reliant on the opinions of others?

- What lie about yourself do you need to cast down to walk with dignity?

Personal Thoughts & Meditations

---

*A*n acronym for fear is **F**alse **E**vidence **A**ppearing **R**eal. As one looks at the world today it is easy to become consumed by fear. Especially if you don't have a firm grip on the Solid Rock, who you must remain anchored to as the shifting sands of time wreak havoc on every element of everyday life. How easy it would be to be reduced to a quivering mass of uncertainty as we listen to the news and the forecasts on global warming, the economy, and the moral issues in today's society. More than ever before we must be certain of who holds tomorrow and be filled with resounding relief that our tomorrows are in the hands of an awesome and all-powerful God!

The certainty of faith comes from belief and hope—and from something that cannot be argued with: experience. The experience that God has shown up before and He will again. When we have been privy to the faithfulness of God, we have an unshakeable foundation in our spirits. We have a testimony in our mouths that chases away fear and questioning. "Will God show up for me?" You know He will because His mercies have been extended to you time and time again! When you have been faithless, God has remained faithful. That is the bottom line and foundation of all you stand on as everything and everyone around you quakes and shakes.

As we walk in fellowship with God, we have His promise that He will reveal what He is about to do to those who draw near to Him. Along with His revelations always comes instruction in order to prepare ourselves for the things to come. As we apply practical wisdom to the spiritual, we are able to rest in the knowledge that we are ready for whatever may occur.

To have a firm grip on your trust in God and be able to laugh at the idle threats of naysayers and doomsday forecasters is liberating. To know that the Lord will supply all your needs according to His riches in glory by Christ Jesus no matter what the Federal Reserve looks like can be a pillow beneath your head as you sleep at night. (See Philippians 4:19.) As Job said, "I know that my Redeemer lives" (Job 19:25). And on that he hung his hat even when he was experiencing the worst trials. He expected God to show up and redeem the time, his pain, and his losses—and God did indeed. Be sure He will do the same for you! So while all others are losing their heads around you, my sister, stand still and see the salvation of the Lord.

Check Yourself

- How prepared are you for the future—emotionally, financially, and physically?

- How do you handle the unexpected? The inconvenient? How does your faith come into play in these circumstances?

- In what circumstances are you more prone to walk in fear? In faith? What is the determining factor for your reaction?

- What is your first response to upsets? What should it be?

- In what ways can you begin to master your reaction to the unexpected?

Personal Thoughts & Meditations

14 Living Wisely

*She speaks with wisdom,
and faithful instruction
is on her tongue.*

PROVERBS 31:26

$\mathcal{W}$hile some wonder why folks won't use the common sense God gave them, I know the answer to this often-asked question: Sense is not common, pure and simple. We are told in the book of James to ask God for wisdom and He will give it to us without scolding or berating us. Wisdom is a precious commodity. Many have traveled far and wide seeking it. Many pay for it as we are assaulted with a plethora of top-dollar seminars, self-empowerment curriculum, how-to literature, and the ever-expanding highway of information—the Internet. Let's face it: Most people are on a quest, seeking answers to their questions.

But we are also told that there is a difference between worldly wisdom and godly wisdom. The wisdom of the world is self-seeking, grounded in flesh, while God's wisdom that comes from above will more than likely demand more than most people are willing to give. Yet God's wisdom is ageless and does more than sound good. It is true, and it works!

My mother always told me as a child that opinions were like noses: Everyone has one, and most don't like theirs. Whether good, bad, ugly, or pretty, everyone has input on any given subject. But the true test is whether what they have to offer holds any lasting virtue. At the end of the day the true test of wisdom affects the environment with positive and lasting change that works to the good of all involved. Does it adhere to the standards of God? And does it give life and nurture wholeness to whom it is imparted?

The Bible tells us in Proverbs chapter 8 that Wisdom was present with God before the world was established. She assisted Him in the details of creation. We are encouraged to seek her early and late. We are told that friendship with Wisdom will bring riches, honor, and long life. But here's my favorite part: Wisdom is personified as a woman. Small wonder we are the nurturers of the universe. We are the givers of sage advice, exhortation, encouragement, and empowerment. Quite a lofty mantle, and yet one that God has entrusted to you and me. In order to wear it well we must do one thing: Seek Him daily for more wisdom.

Check Yourself

- Do others seek you out for advice?

- What is your advice based on? Is it helpful to others?

- In what ways do you seek to bring understanding to those who need it?

- What is your response when you see others doing things that could be harmful to them?

- How much do you listen before you give advice? Do the recipients of your advice usually feel as if you're really empathetic? How do they receive your advice?

Personal Thoughts & Meditations

I have studied the way Jesus interacted with those who came to Him seeking advice. I've sought to incorporate His techniques into my life. The first thing that struck me about His conversation was that it was riddled with questions as opposed to just stating His opinion. I pondered this long and hard, and then the wisdom of it began to bring light to my understanding. I have long been a person who had strong opinions, and I have been more than happy to share them whether I was invited to or not. But it was through a painful series of events that I finally learned to wait until my opinion was asked for. But the greater lesson came when I learned to ask more questions and not move forward in haste, to probe until I had a greater understanding of the situation. I also now wait until the people seeking advice gain clarity for themselves. By asking leading questions, I help them get a clearer view for themselves and come to a healthy conclusion. You see, I learned that I could not convince anyone to change just based on what I thought. But when I empowered them to see their own circumstance objectively, they were then liberated to make the right choices and secure the change they desired. This was what Jesus did. He took the time to allow people to see the state of their own hearts as they spoke with

Him. As the light came on in their hearts, it was the seekers who began to see the need for change.

Truly, for most of us women the urgency to set a situation right propels us to speak before we think. Oftentimes we're met with resistance to our counsel. But true wisdom marries itself with kindness and empathy and takes the time to be heard, understood, and better yet, received. Do try this questioning technique at home.

Check Yourself

- How discerning are you about when to speak and when to be silent?

- Do you react first and think later? Do you allow others the freedom to heed or ignore your counsel?

- Does your advice come from a place of judgment or compassion? How are you able to remain impartial?

- In what ways do you put others at peace when offering advice?

- Why is kindness crucial to the process of giving counsel?

Personal Thoughts & Meditations

The world tells us that a good man is hard to find, but the Word tells us a faithful man is even more difficult to locate. Faithfulness, though an admirable trait, is difficult to master because it goes against the grain of our humanity. We are fickle by nature and given to change. Though we crave security, we are delightfully distracted by variety. The art of remaining true to our commitments escapes us as we trip over our own flesh. Yet in the midst of this God remains faithful to us. He stands beside us in our weakness, ready and willing to restore us no matter how distasteful our mistakes and failings. Even with God's magnificent example, we still struggle with those in our lives who fall below the standard we set for them.

Though we all seek grace, we sometimes struggle to give it. Yet grace is an important factor in relationships. The ability to patiently and faithfully love others through their disappointing behavior and untimely outbursts makes us more approachable and accessible. Our company is more often sought if it is known that our friendship comes without judgment, conditions, or schedules for redemption. Though we speak the truth, it is saturated with love and grace. In this manner we become havens of rest to our loved ones, an oasis in a land where many wander thirsty for a kind word, a drink of hope, a shower of restoration.

Who can find a friend so faithful? Jesus becomes the ultimate example. Loving us, living for us, dying for us, taking up our part in the midst of our weakness. If we could only purpose to walk in this way toward those we love we would reap the reward of rich and enduring relationships. Being true to our commitments is a way of honoring the relationships God has given us. In this way we exhibit His vast and timeless love toward us and glorify Him as a faithful Father, bringing a smile to His face and favor to our own lives.

Check Yourself

- How faithful are you to going through the process with others?

- What types of things make you impatient with others?

- In the midst of your own struggles, what is important for you to receive from others?

- What must you be mindful of when walking with others through their struggles?

- What is the mind-set of God when dealing with us in our shortcomings? How can we apply ourselves to persevering with others?

Personal Thoughts & Meditations

15 Achieving Balance

*She watches over
the affairs of her household
and does not eat the bread
of idleness.*

PROVERBS 31:27

Sassy

The woman who sang about the fact that she could bring home the bacon, fry it up in a pan, and never let her man forget he was a man didn't look any worse for wear as she sang her song and pranced across the television screen to promote the womanly fragrance Enjoli. However, you better believe that television land is a far cry from the reality that most women inhabit. How to find balance is the big mystery. As more women have entered the workforce than ever before, some have found that their priorities still emanate from the heart first. Thus comes the movement of women leaving the marketplace and returning home. Not all of us can do this based on economic needs or the fact that we truly do feel called to function in a career. What then? How do we find the balance between home and the outside demands that must also be addressed? First, nurturing a close relationship with God. Then communication and commitment to the needs of your family. After that comes everyone else. I once heard one of my mentors say she couldn't be "out in the world ministering to others" while her family went to hell. Because of this belief she restructured her life accordingly. Interestingly enough, her family began to thrive as never before. Broken relationships were restored, her children began to live in harmony with the Word of God, and her husband began to excel and the work of his hands were blessed. As for her, the things she had planted in her career sector began to grow and prosper her on a greater level without her having to overlook every detail.

I believe the secret to her success was scheduling time with her family, creating special rituals that made each one feel special, and even scheduling times of rest. There were times when the phone would not be answered because it was family time. This requires great discipline, but the end result is sounder minds and bodies that are up to meeting the challenges of everyday living because the time was taken to recalibrate. We will stand before God individually to give account for our time, our priorities, and the stewardship of all He entrusted to our care. And the most precious priorities are God and our families.

Check Yourself

- How plugged into your home are you? What distracts you from being more grounded?

- How busy are you? Is your busyness just activity or is it fruitful? In what ways?

- What could you eliminate from your schedule? What do you need to add?

- How does being overscheduled affect a household?

- In what ways can you nurture more together time in your home?

Personal Thoughts & Meditations

ecently a friend shared with me that she had just found out that her husband had been having an affair for several years. Everyone knew about it but her. I wondered where she had been. Why didn't she know something was wrong? Something about his pattern had to have changed and given her warning. At some point his absence and emotional distance had to become noticeable. And yet if her life was a whirlwind, she probably welcomed his lack of affection and attention because she already had far too much on her plate. The high cost of doing far too much business is that we are losing our families in the shuffle of over-packed schedules. We must face a serious question. We must consider why our schedules are so packed and what we are trying to achieve. It's time to determine what is truly important at the end of the day. A sound family environment that is a respite from the storm outside to everyone in the household and all who visit perhaps? Then we must return to the days of a simpler life. This can only occur through establishing order in your home. This may sound simplistic, but having a schedule that includes everyone creates a feeling of cohesive community.

This atmosphere helps your children learn accountability and the importance of honoring authority. Your husband should be made to feel like a king and you his reigning queen in this mini kingdom that prepares your children for the world at large while offering safety from all that assaults their faith, their sensibilities, and their identities. This should be the place where relationship secures the fiber of who they grow to be as people. This should be the place where you find safety in the arms of your husband, and he finds nurturing and rest in yours.

If you are single this is the place that becomes your sanctuary, with or without children or pets. You have the awesome privilege of creating a feeling of community in your home as well by including your circle of friends and family in rituals that you establish. Home is where all should feel welcome and secure while you find your refreshing and sustenance within its walls. This is the environment in which God blesses your relationships and strengthens and fortifies your soul to equip you for facing the world outside your door. He knows that victorious living begins at home.

Check Yourself

- How watchful are you over the heart condition of your loved ones? Are you sensitive to their emotions and struggles?

- How cognizant are you of their schedules, of their patterns of movement and activity? In what ways do you keep track of everyone's commitments?

- Would you notice if something were wrong even if they didn't tell you? How?

- In what ways do you stay in touch with your children? Your mate? Your friends?

- How do you set the open communication atmosphere in your home?

Personal Thoughts & Meditations

———————————

*I*t's ten o'clock. Do you know where your children are?" Back in the day when curfews were strictly enforced this was a familiar line. Sad to say, today most parents would probably answer no. Knowing what is going on with everyone in your household—keeping up with all the various schedules and goings on—has become almost impossible.

Parents and children are overcommitted. Johnny has football practice on Monday, debate team on Tuesday, swimming on Wednesday, journalism club on Thursday, something else on Friday, a packed day on Saturday, and he collapses on Sunday, too exhausted to pay attention and certainly not interested in going to church.

If he is not of driving age, you too are exhausted from picking up and dropping him off, along with your own hectic schedule. And we haven't even gotten to your husband, making meals, cleaning the house, and your job! Small wonder everyone is stressed, angry, and burned out. We all retreat to our separate rooms, seeking our own space. Dinnertime as a family has become a dinosaur on the other side of extinction. We don't know half our children's friends and where they go after we've made a drop. Nonexistent family life is an explosion waiting to happen.

As mothers we are called to nurture our children and guard jealously over their destinies and their spiritual inheritance. These things cannot be accomplished if we are having long-distance relationships with our children. In the scheme of things, sacrifices have to be made to honor the season we are called mothers before we can transition to be friends of our children.

The first rule of thumb is to help our children learn to prioritize by not allowing them to be involved in a hundred things at the same time. Limiting how many activities they can be involved in during a semester teaches them to make choices and remain committed to them. Many workforce managers today complain that workers entering the marketplace are unable to make decisions. Help your kids develop that skill. And only allow as much activity as you can keep track of comfortably.

Taking the time to eat together and stay in touch not just physically but also emotionally and spiritually is important to keeping your finger on the pulse of where your children are. Listen without interjecting so you can really hear what's going on with them. Making your house a haven for them and their friends is also a way of staying in tune. And last but not least, establish open access—none of this "their room is off limits" to you stuff. I don't believe children should have privacy until they can pay their own rent or mortgage.

Remember that in this season of parenting, you must be a parent first. You can be a friend later when they have matured to the place of honoring you and seeking you on another level because their needs have changed. Do you know where your children are? God has given you charge of these lives to mold them in a way that brings glory to Him. Be a wise and firm steward.

Check Yourself

- What is the difference between being busy and being effective in your home?

- What should the criteria be for whether an activity is added to your schedule or not?

- How can you help your children learn how to prioritize and make choices they will remain committed to?

- What are signs of overload for you? For your children?

- Why is balance so important in a household? How does lack of rest affect your ability to perform?

- At the end of the day do you have a sense of accomplishment? Why or why not? If you don't, what changes do you need to make for this to occur?

Personal Thoughts & Meditations

16 Building Up Others

Her children arise
and call her blessed;
her husband also, and he praises her:
"Many women do noble things,
but you surpass them all."

PROVERBS 31:28-29

grew up according to the rule that children should be seen and not heard. Perhaps that's why so many of us from my generation had issues later in life. Parents need to hear their children—hear their hearts and discern their spirits. The world has changed, and the pressures that today's children endure is unfathomable. In the fast-moving world of technology where the Internet is replacing one-on-one relationships and luring some kids into severe danger, it is more important than ever to place our ears to hear the heartbeat of our children.

The Bible tells us that a child comes into the world seeking correction. Let us not disappoint them. In my mind I get a picture of a brand-new computer that I just purchased. It sits on my desk awaiting the right programs. As I download specific ones, it performs according to its operating capabilities. The computer takes on the mind of the programmer and the programs. The same with children. They come into the world with no instructions, but as we begin to teach them right, from day one, they literally take on our mind-set. Their decisions are ruled according to what we teach them, just as we learn the Word of God and develop the mind of Christ. It's the same principle. This is why it's important to note that whatever holes you leave in your children's foundation will be filled in by information from their peers.

But just as they hear *us* they must be heard *by* us. They must feel as if they have a safe place to submit their questions and fears and be given sound answers and reassurance free of chastisement and judgment. This is the delicate balance of being a parent—being honored as the authority and being the one who can be confided in. It is not realistic to think your children will confide everything to you. But they should feel safe enough to tell you the things that might have a lasting effect on their lives. You will be relied on to guide their choices. And in some things there will even be a sense of relief for what you do not allow. You are their safety net. How ironic are the tales of countless children who were indulged and spoiled—and later say their parents didn't love them. Far above material gifts and allowing them to run amuck, the proof of your love to a child is the extent of your personal involvement and discipline.

Check Yourself

- What is your children's attitude toward you? How do they express this to you?

- What type of relationship do you have with your children?

- In what ways do you honor your children? In what ways do they honor you?

- In what ways do you seek to be a true parent to your children?

- How would you describe your friendship with your children? How do you balance your parent/friend relationship?

Personal Thoughts & Meditations

---

*J*ust as a wife is a reflection of the success and nurturing of her husband, so is the husband a mirror of the care and influence of his wife. In essence a woman has the power to build up or destroy her man in countless ways. She also has the awesome capacity to so inspire her man to be his best for her that in doing so he becomes a credit to his household and his community.

The words she whispers to him late in the midnight hour. The way she touches his shoulder in quiet reassurance. The light of love and admiration that shines in her eyes that causes his chest to swell with confidence. Her cooperation that makes him feel as if he is on a strong team. The knowledge that he is not in the war alone, that his woman has his back and wants the best for him. All these things, as subtle as they may be, become benchmarks in a man's spirit that help make him the man who faces the world for all to see.

Yes, it is true. As God ordained woman to be the helpmeet

of man, her touch can make the difference in his character and integrity. A man lives to be a success in the eyes of his woman. When she praises him it spurs him on to higher heights. When she criticizes him the failure he feels is immeasurable. Depending on the weight of it, he can either abdicate his place as husband, protector, and provider or seek to dominate through oppression to secure the space his spirit is wired to occupy.

The power of a woman can help her man scale the walls of his own spirit to reach God. To stretch out his arms in protective prayer. To extend hands to caress her and correct his children. All this is hidden within her prayer closet and the words of her heart. It is also released in the atmosphere she sets in their home. Her willingness to minister to his soul, mind, spirit, and body give him a joy and desire to do more to bring a smile to her face and greater depths of love to her heart.

Behind every great man is a great woman who has planted seeds of greatness in his spirit that release him to release her into her own levels of greatness. Together they become a true picture of Christ and the church. Husband and wife united as one to the pleasure of the Father.

Check Yourself

- If your husband had to give a review of you as a wife, what would he say? If you're single, what would the men in your life have to say about you?

- What would you like your husband to say about you?

- What would you have to do to get him to say these things?

- In what ways do you seek to surpass your mate's expectations of you?

- How important is the blessing of your husband to you? In what ways does this empower you as a woman?

Personal Thoughts & Meditations

_____

*J*esus, as He left the disciples, told them that greater things would they do than the acts He performed (John 14:12). If we follow the biblical template of the older women teaching the younger women how to love their husbands, we should see a generation of women coming to the forefront who raise the standard of loving their husbands, raising their children, and reaching out to the community with charitable acts of kindness.

Many women transcend the typical notion of women. They're free enough to love their sisters around them without pretense or jealousy. They live by example, setting a standard without saying a word. These women are like Deborah in the book of Judges, who led a nation but still knew to leave the physical fighting to the men. Women like Lydia, who balanced her success in the marketplace with leaving a mark in the kingdom by being on her knees. Or like Anna the prophetess, who knew how to hold on to faith until she saw her desire manifested. And Esther, who decided after prayer and fasting that the way to save a nation was through her ministry as a wife to her husband. These are women set apart who surpassed those around them because of their dedication to their God, their family, their community.

The power of passion to live up to the calling of God is the greatest motivator to bring Him glory while ministering to the needs of those He has placed in our midst. We can leave a lasting impact on those who had needs before they met us and found themselves filled while walking with us. Oh to be like Tabitha, who blessed a circle of women so they literally mourned her back to life by rehearsing her deeds to the apostle Peter who, compelled by their tears, raised her from the dead through his prayers to God on her behalf. To live on in the hearts of your friends and family will be the distinguishing mark of your accomplishments. The final punctuation being your entrance into the heavenlies where Jesus waits to receive you and grant you rest. And at the end of all your days you will look back with gladness, knowing that every thought and deed of service was well worth it.

Check Yourself

- In what ways would you like to excel in your interactions with your loved ones? Who is someone you would like to model your life after?

- What acts of service do you find joy in?

- What sets you apart from others in your circle of friends?

- What gifts do you contribute to your inner circle that enriches their lives?

- What things have you been praised for among your friends?

Personal Thoughts & Meditations

17 *Inner Strength*

*Charm is deceptive, and
beauty is fleeting;
but a woman who
fears the LORD is to be praised.*

PROVERBS 31:30

Sassy

othing is sadder than witnessing a faded starlet who no longer knows how to navigate through the waters of life because she can no longer manipulate the oars she once used. We watch her flail beneath the lines that time has etched across her face and the folds that have settled into her body, humbling her and forcing her to extend graces instead of a perfectly manicured hand to get her way. Her looks no longer hold the power they once possessed to send others quickly panting in pursuit of her wishes. And so she hesitates, broken by time and its effects on what was once considered unattainable perfection. Humbled by her lack of external power, she searches for power from within but finds nothing more than undeveloped hints at character that never saw the light of day because it didn't have to.

People can be rendered quite helpless when the tools of charm and manipulation no longer work. Like Jezebel, who painted her face and winked at the general coming to town from her tower hoping to hinder her fate of being dethroned, the shock of finding yourself among the dogs when you were once untouchable can be a rude awakening.

Juxtapose this against the picture of a woman secure in who she is because she rests in the arms of God. Fearing no one except her heavenly King, she rises to each occasion, knowing she has the favor of God resting on her like a warm mantle shielding her from the coldness of refusal. She knows her fate lies in the hands of the One who holds her future secure, and she's bookmarked between goodness and mercy. And because of what she receives she is able to give grace for grace, seeking no return from those she extends her hands to. Her gaze remains heavenward, awaiting her reward from the One who has the deepest of unending resources—resources she freely dispenses, buoyed by the understanding that she has been blessed for a purpose—to be a greater blessing to others.

Check Yourself

- How much do you rely on charm to get you what you want? How much do you rely on your beauty?

- In what ways do your charm and beauty work for you? Can they always be relied on to get you what you want?

- How does your character measure up to your charm and beauty?

- Which areas of your character would you focus on developing if you were not attractive?

- What is the definition of inner beauty to you? How can it be more attractive than the external?

Personal Thoughts & Meditations

J have always found it interesting that though the world does not embrace Christ, the general masses most certainly know how Christians should behave. And oh how disappointed they are when we fall beneath that standard. Harsh and unforgiving, they use the failures of man to rail against a flawless God. Whenever this occurs I am once again reminded of the awesome responsibility I have as one who walks in relationship with Christ to glorify Him in everything I say and do. Once again I am made more aware that I don't represent myself. To some people we are the only Bible they will ever read as they examine the pages of our lives.

How we respond to the issues of life will be most telling of whom we serve—either ourselves or the One who orchestrates the movements of the stars in the heavens that hang suspended above. Know that you will be corrected lest you forget yourself in one of those moments that squeezes a remnant of flesh forgotten or ignored from your inner being. Pressure reveals who we are faster than anything else. And our humanity can be inconvenient in the face of those who are harsher judges because they are unfamiliar with the grace of God. We are called to a higher standard of living and responding if we are to be a credit to God.

A woman who fears the Lord brings a unique element into every environment she enters. The atmosphere should change. People should apologize if they cursed. Raucous behavior should calm. Ribald actions should be put on reserve. Not because of anything you say or do but simply because you are you—an agent of God carrying His Spirit within you. There should be something different about you. An evident grace. Something that sets you apart. An unspeakable difference that is perceived but cannot be explained.

Because we walk in absolute surrender to God, we bring peace to troubled waters. Sound judgment to confusion. Prudence to carelessness. Discernment to foolishness. Of course, we're not perfected in a day. As experience becomes our teacher in the daily routines of life, we become like diamonds in the hands of God as He shapes and polishes us to perfection and then holds us forth as beautiful examples of His love and transformation power. And in the beautiful display lies a glimmer of hope bright enough to become contagious to all who see it, revealing that they too can be transformed into vessels of honor.

Check Yourself

- How much do those around you know about your relationship with the Lord?

- How does your attitude toward God affect the way you carry yourself?

- When considering your choices, what motivates your decisions?

- What are you known for among your peers? How does it affect their behavior around you?

- In what ways does your reputation for godliness precede you?

Personal Thoughts & Meditations

---

*M*y generation laughs about the fact that as children we don't know who we feared most—our mothers or God. All we know is that we were definitely scared straight. We were scared of following the crowd to do what we knew was wrong because we were more afraid of facing our mothers and God than falling prey to peer pressure. And this was a good thing. It is true. Fear of the Lord is the beginning of wisdom because it is in light of that awesome respect for the heart of God that His keeping power becomes a grace on our lives.

As I've watched those who have been caught doing wrong repent, only to be asked if they were sorry because they got caught or because they were truly sorry, I see the light shift in their eyes and realize it is the consequences of their actions that hurt them more than the realization of their fallen nature. When we consider the love of God and all He sacrificed for us to be reconciled to Himself, it should be enough to reduce us to trembling surrender and a hatred for doing anything that would offend Him. Lest your perception be skewed to perceive of God as some soft-hearted monarch who will overlook your offenses, consider the other side of God. The side that is all-powerful, majestic, and able to wield judgment. The side of Him that hates sin because it lives outside His holiness and cannot enter into His presence. It is this sin that separates us from what He loves and longs after most—us.

As we stand in awe and reverence for Him, our impulses are transformed in the light of longing to be close to Him. We begin to hate what He hates and love what He loves. Love burns in our hearts, causing us to hunger after righteousness and yield in joyous submission to our King. The peace that surrounds us draws others so that we might point the way to Him. Like beacons set on a hill, we forge a trail through the darkness, revealing a path that leads from slavery to liberty, causing many to sing, "He who the Son sets free is free indeed." This is when we become ever so thankful for that wholesome fear of God liberating us from fearful oppression and giving us wings to fly above the fray of life and all that hinders us from living our best life right here, right now.

Check Yourself

- How can the fear of the Lord cause you to make wise decisions?

- How can your fear of the Lord positively affect those around you?

- In what ways can a relationship with God enhance your life and bring you honor?

- What is the difference between those who reverence the Word of God and those who live according to their own design?

- Why is the one who refuses to honor God considered a fool in Scripture?

Personal Thoughts & Meditations

18

Generosity

Give her the reward
she has earned, and
let her works bring
her praise at the city gate.

PROVERBS 31:31

Though you may look for a return for all that you have done for others, don't make the mistake of looking for fruit where you planted seed. Roots travel, my friend, and seldom come up where you expect. This is crucial to your understanding lest you grow disappointed and bitter. Whatever you do, do it unto God. Do it for His sake, and you will always serve with pleasure.

One day God spoke to me and told me I had become selfish. I was appalled by this disclosure and asked Him why He would accuse me of such a thing. I considered myself quite generous in nature. It was then that He opened my eyes to see that for a long time I had given out of fear and insecurity. It started as a young child when I was insecure in a new neighborhood and country. In order to secure new friends I gave away valuable items that had been given to me, hoping for acceptance. This attitude continued to adulthood but was thinly veiled beneath my Christian heart...or so I thought until God revealed to me the motivation of my giving. "You don't believe that anyone could love you just for you," He said. I was mortified. It was true. I was afraid to stand alone, naked in my giftlessness, fearing rejection if I had nothing more to offer than myself.

In light of this revelation I began to examine my motives for everything I did for others. If I found my giving attached to an expectation of a return, I refrained from giving until I could give simply for the pleasure of giving. I found that the more I gave, the more my joy increased. And it was not just in things, I relished giving *myself* to others. I came to recognize this was the greatest gift I could give. As Jesus gave His life, I want to be remembered for giving mine. If in any way my words, a hug, a nudge to laughter could encourage someone to go one step farther, to reach a little higher, to come closer to God, to love her husband more, to become the best she can be, then my life will not have been in vain. It is my passion, my purpose, my highest goal to make a lasting difference in the lives of everyone I encounter face-to-face or by any other means. May we all live out our purpose to the glory of God!

Check Yourself

- What would you like your epitaph to say?

- What works would you like to be remembered for?

- What do you do to prompt praise from those around you?

- How do you practice giving of yourself to those you love?

- What legacy are you perfecting in your day-to-day now?

Personal Thoughts & Meditations

I am sure you would say the same thing if we were in a conversation, but I am mystified that each of my friends has profoundly different personalities. It is the uniqueness of their personas that drew me to them, and through them I live vicariously, sampling different facets and flavors of life through their experiences. Life is fuller because of them and all they bring to my life.

Like a bowl of party mix, my friends bring delight in different ways—some bittersweet, some just sweet, but always interesting and full of surprises. Sometimes it has been in the silent moments shared with friends that amazing revelations have come. Sometimes the experience has been painful exposure when confronted with a truth I didn't want to hear—and yet it was good medicine that later healed me as I took it in and let it do its work.

As I ponder the effect that my friends have had on my life, I only hope to leave as deep an impression on them as they have left on me. I believe that we were all created to rub against one another until the rough edges are made so smooth that we can fit nicely into the Master's hand and be used to fell giants who choose to rise up against the people of God and all that God's kingdom stands for.

The impact of walking together, sustaining one another's faith, and holding one another accountable leaves lines on our spirits that cannot be erased. These deep impressions stand the test of time and effect lasting change in the lives of those who surround us as they witness our growth and transformation. You and I are living testaments merging together in one lifetime that tell the story of divine love and salvation and leave the evidence that we were here and our lives matter more than we can ever know.

Check Yourself

- What lasting thing about your personality would you like others to remember and honor you for?

- What would be the greatest reward in your mind for a life well lived?

- What would a photograph of your life depict?

- What would your deeds declare about you?

- What would be the one thing everyone would celebrate you for?

Personal Thoughts & Meditations

———————

One day we will all stand before God. All we've ever done will speak for us in heaven as well as on earth. Our works will tell stories of encounters of struggle, tales of surrender, and acts of selflessness. Some stories will be praiseworthy and some will not. And yet we select the content for the volumes that will be told by how we live our lives, by the choices we make, and by the degrees we allow our flesh to die so the Spirit of God can reign in us.

Our works will speak of time well spent and time lost on wasted pleasures that bore no lasting fruit. They will reveal how much time was spent in prayer or lost on the efforts of fleshly wrestling. Our works will declare tales of victory as well as the anguish of defeats we wish could be erased. But the most comforting thing our works will share is the greater work that Christ accomplished for us and through us.

It is this tale that will erase all other stories that don't bear repeating once we stand before Him and revel in the fulfillment of the greatest work of all—that of His saving grace.

Check Yourself

- When you stand before God, what would you like to show Him about your life?

- What would you like Him to say about your life?

- What do you need to do in order for Him to say that?

- What do you think would delight Him most about your life?

- What would you like your reputation in heaven to be?

Personal Thoughts & Meditations

Master Checklist

On a scale of 1 to 5, with 1 being best, rank how you're doing in these areas. After each area give three things you can do to improve.

_____ Excellence—

_____ Discretion—

_____ Resourcefulness—

_____ Diligence—

_____ Discipline—

_____ Creativity—

_____ Wisdom—

_____ Prudence—

_____ Strength—

_____ Savvy—

_____ Generosity—

_____ Benevolence—

_____ Style—

_____ Conviction—

_____ Faith—

_____ Knowledge—

_____ Faithfulness—

_____ Character—

_____ Integrity—

_____ Honor—

To contact Michelle or to book her
for a speaking engagement, write to

HeartWing Ministries
PO Box 11052
Chicago, IL 60611

or log on to

www.michellehammond.com

or call

866-391-0955

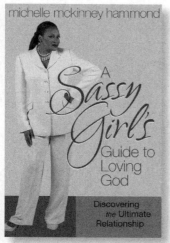

Sassy Girl's Guide to Loving God

Michelle McKinney Hammond

"Ultimately our love for God affects every area of our lives," bestselling author Michelle McKinney Hammond writes, "from our prayer life to how we look at the world at large." Encouraging you to return to the joy and passion of your early walk, *A Sassy Girl's Guide to Loving God* shows how you can...

- keep your prayer line open for communication with God

- build your faith by embracing the promises of the Bible

- obey God's commands with a cheerful heart that is open to change

If you've grown dry in your faith or desire a closer walk with Jesus, you will receive practical inspiration for igniting the spark in your heart. You'll also gain renewed hope and more excitement as you totally embrace the heartbeat of God.

Sassy, Single, and Satisfied

Michelle McKinney Hammond

If you're single, this book is for you! This delightful devotional helps you explore your place in the world and draw closer to the true Lover of your soul. With joy and love, Michelle McKinney Hammond combines usable scriptural principles for daily living with inspirational stories, quotes, and personal experiences of life, love, and men.

Sassy, Single, and Satisfied encourages you to embrace and celebrate this season of singleness. You will also discover how to...

- align your priorities
- get the most from being single
- have a joyful and meaningful existence

With her humorous, tell-it-like-it-is style, Michelle shares the ups and downs of singleness, helps you accentuate the positives, and reveals the fulfillment you can find in Christ.